AF207604

No Promises in the Wind

by
Irene Hunt

Teacher Guide

Written by
Phyllis A. Green

Note

The Berkley/Pacer paperback edition of the book was used to prepare this guide. The page references may differ in other editions.

Please note: Please assess the appropriateness of this book for the age level and maturity of your students prior to reading and discussing it with your class.

ISBN 1-56137-739-2

To order, contact your local school supply store, or—

Novel Units, Inc.
P.O. Box 97
Bulverde, TX 78163-0097

Web site: www.educyberstor.com

Table of Contents

Skills and Strategies

Thinking
Brainstorming, classifying,
research, decision-making

Comprehension
Predicting, inference,
comparison/contrast

Writing
Opinion, defining, naming,
letter-writing

Vocabulary
Antonyms/synonyms,
prefixes/suffixes

Listening/Speaking
Sounds, drama

Literary Elements
Mood, character analysis,
conflict, story mapping

Summary of *No Promises in the Wind*

1932 in America was the depth of the Depression and just eating and surviving were hard. The Grondowski Family has fallen on hard times, the father is out of work, the mother does ironing to keep food on the table (barely), Kitty loses her office job, Josh delivers papers before going to school, and Joey is just hungry. The natural tensions of the situation cause Josh, age fifteen, to take to the road. Ten-year-old Joey accompanies him along with his friend Howie. Howie is killed shortly after in a railroad accident. The brothers persevere and work in a carnival for a period, but when a fire destroys the carnival operation, they make their way to Nebraska to Lonnie, a truck driver who had befriended them. The boys are separated when they quarrel over a half loaf of bread and Joey leaves. Though both are seriously ill, they are reunited and convalesce in Lonnie's home. They find work at a local restaurant as musical entertainers and eventually return to Chicago and their parents.

About the Author

Irene Hunt was born and raised in Illinois. She attended the University of Illinois, A.B. 1939 and the University of Minnesota, M.A. 1946. She taught French and English, 1930-1945 in the Oak Park, Illinois public schools. Between 1946 and 1950 she taught at the University of South Dakota. Ms. Hunt returned to Illinois to act as a teacher and consultant in the Cicero, Illinois public schools.

Irene Hunt received the Charles W. Follett Award in 1964, the American Notable Book Award in 1965, and was the sole runner-up for the Newbery Medal, 1965, for *Across Five Aprils*. In 1967 she received the Newbery Medal for *Up a Road Slowly.*

Other Books by Irene Hunt:
The Everlasting Hills, The Lottery Rose (Novel Unit available), *Up a Road Slowly*, and *Across Five Aprils* (Novel Unit available)

Initiating Activities

(Several possibilities are listed. Choose for your particular class.)
1. The book is set in 1932 in America. What do you know of that time? What do you expect? Record what you know in the "K" column and what you expect in the "E" column. Return to the "W" column to record what you've learned after you read.

What They Know	What They would Like to Know	What They Learned

2. Free-write your feelings if you were fifteen and your father was out of work and angry, lunch was an oleo sandwich, you had a three-hour paper route before school to help out the family, and you wanted to enjoy and develop your musical talent.

3. Look over the cover, the summary on the back cover, and the illustrations. What are your predictions for the book?

4. Consider these facts from the story: a banjo, piano-playing ability, and two brothers aged ten and fifteen on the road. What are your predictions for their fate and what may be included in the book?

5. Read aloud the first seven pages of the book, ending with "patient." Start to fill in a story map with what you've discovered about the book so far. Make some predictions for the conflict in the story. Read on.

Vocabulary Activities

Teacher Note: It is suggested that vocabulary activities be included in each day's instructional time.

1. Prefixes and Suffixes: Look for these prefixes among the vocabulary words (des-, com-, in-, ab-, e-, mono-, non-, in-, mis-, con-). Identify the words, use them in sentences, and then define the prefix. Do the same for these suffixes (-ery, -ous, -ion, -ity, -ious).

2. Choose six important incidents to summarize the action in the story. Get a notion of the mood of each incident and choose a noun, an adjective, and an adverb to typify the incidents.

Incident	Noun	Adjective	Adverb

3. See page 11 of this guide for a 5 x 5 matrix for Vocabulary Bingo. On the 5 x 5 matrix, students fill in vocabulary words. To call the bingo squares, students prepare definitions, recording them on cards. Encourage "crossword puzzle" kinds of clues.

4. Create some gradation strings for the words. On the string include words with similar definition, differing only in degree; e.g., like, enjoy, adore, love.

5. Display the vocabulary words on a word wall (with words on sentence strips in the manner of bricks). Pairs of students pick up the challenge to get the partner to say words from the wall with short definitions, within time limits.

6. Make a vocabulary cube for extra credit at the conclusion of lessons. Each of the six faces of the cube offer what to do with given vocabulary words—use in a sentence, synonym, antonym, etymology, define, and part of speech. The teacher tosses the cube to a student who must react to the word in whatever way is requested on the cube's face, where he catches the cube.

7. Provide short phrases to explain selected vocabulary words to an alien who has come to earth and wants to explain words and objects in an intergalactic museum. For example, a bridge would be a road over water.

8. Connect two or three of the vocabulary words. From a list of words, the student chooses two or three to connect and explain. For example, in chapter one, *scorning* and *rancor* go together because they might be used in a description of an argument. Here's the pattern: _____ and _____ go together because _____.

9. Use some of the words in figurative language. Similes are comparisons using "like" or "as." Metaphors are comparisons without "like" or "as." Personification gives human traits and mannerisms to inanimate objects. Hyperbole is extreme exaggeration.

10. Sort the words from several chapters, creating your own attribute web or other word map.

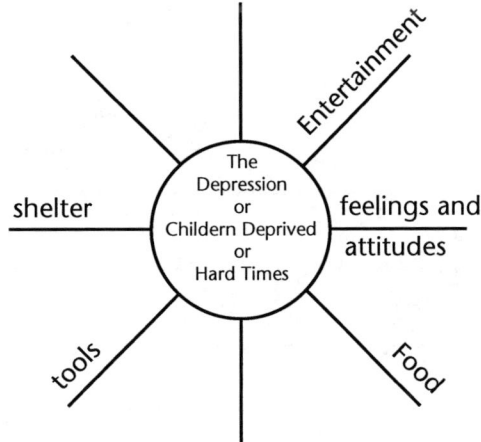

Using Predictions in the Novel Unit Approach

We all make predictions as we read—little guesses about what will happen next, how the conflict will be resolved, which details given by the author will be important to the plot, which details will help to fill in our sense of a character. Students should be encouraged to predict, to make sensible guesses. As students work on predictions, these discussion questions can be used to guide them: What are some of the ways to predict? What is the process of a sophisticated reader's thinking and predicting? What clues does an author give us to help us in making our predictions? Why are some predictions more likely than others?

A predicting chart is for students to record their predictions. As each subsequent chapter is discussed, you can review and correct previous predictions. This procedure serves to focus on predictions and to review the stories.

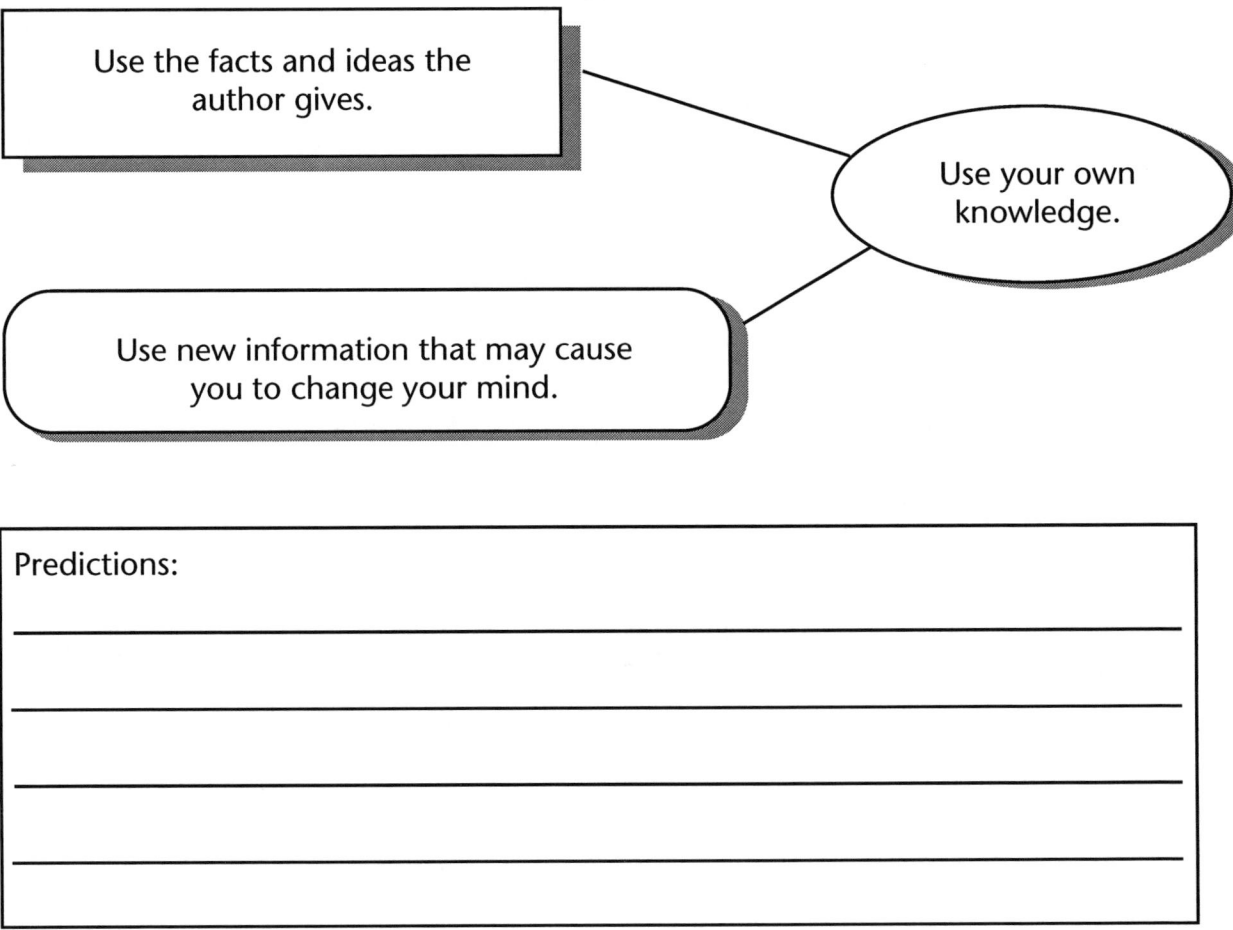

Use the facts and ideas the author gives.

Use your own knowledge.

Use new information that may cause you to change your mind.

Predictions:

_____

_____

_____

_____

Prediction Chart

What characters have we met so far?	What is the conflict in the story?	What are your predictions?	Why did you make those predictions?

Story Map

Setting

↓

Problem

↓

Goal

↓

Episodes

↓

Resolution

Characters_____

_____

_____

_____

Time and Place_____

_____

_____

_____

Beginning ——→ Development ——→ Outcome

_____

_____

_____

_____

_____

_____

_____

Using Character Webs—In the Novel Unit Approach

Attribute Webs are simply a visual representation of a character from the novel. They provide a systematic way for the students to organize and recap the information they have about a particular character. Attribute webs may be used after reading the novel to recapitulate information about a particular character or completed gradually as information unfolds, done individually, or finished as a group project.

One type of character attribute web uses these divisions:

● How a character acts and feels. (How does the character feel in this picture? How would you feel if this happened to you? How do you think the character feels?)

● How a character looks. (Close your eyes and picture the character. Describe him to me.)

● Where a character lives. (Where and when does the character live?)

● How others feel about the character. (How does another specific character feel about our character?)

In group discussion about the student attribute webs and specific characters, the teacher can ask for backup proof from the novel. You can also include inferential thinking.

Attribute webs need not be confined to characters. They may also be used to organize information about a concept, object or place.

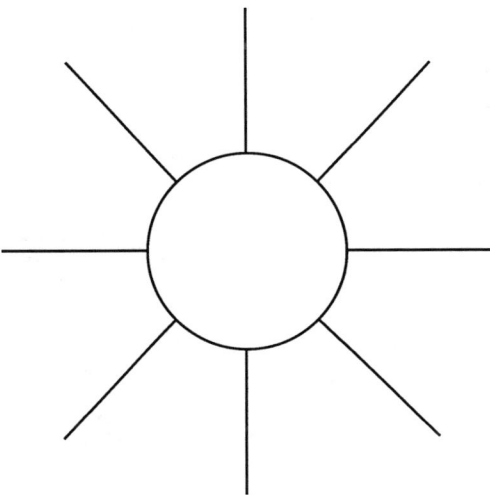

9

Attribute Web

The attribute web below is designed to help you gather clues the author provides about what a character is like. Fill in the blanks with words and phrases which tell how the character acts and looks, as well as what the character says and what others say about him or her.

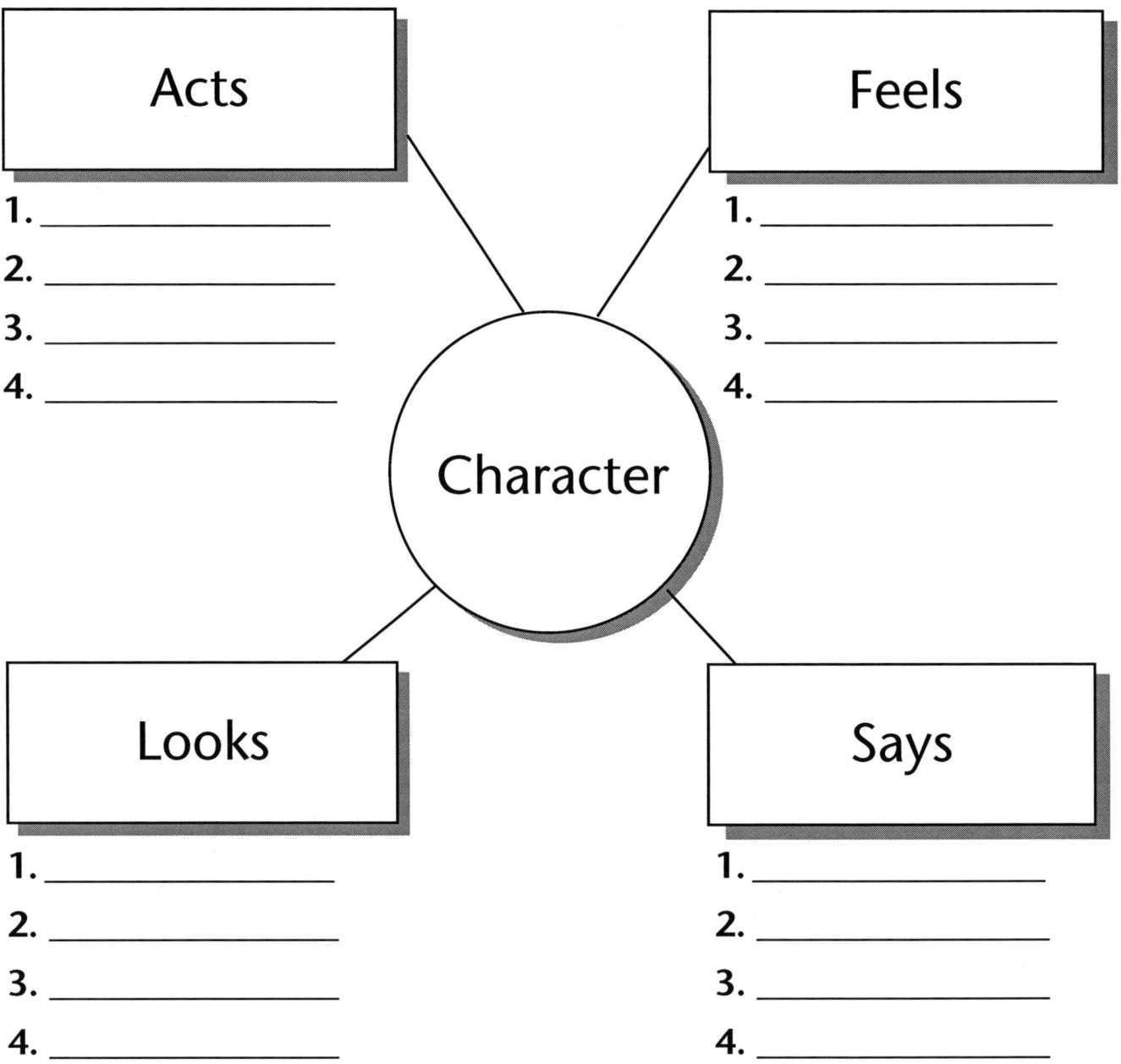

Acts

1. _____
2. _____
3. _____
4. _____

Feels

1. _____
2. _____
3. _____
4. _____

Character

Looks

1. _____
2. _____
3. _____
4. _____

Says

1. _____
2. _____
3. _____
4. _____

Vocabulary Bingo

Chapter One—Pages 7-30

Plot Summary:

It is 1932 in Chicago and the storyteller, Josh, age 15, whose dad has lost his job, his older sister has been laid off, his younger brother is sickly, and his mother irons to put food on the table, decides to leave home. He clashes strongly with his father, a proud but broken man, who finds fault with most of what Josh says and does.

Vocabulary:

scorning 8	roused 8	calloused 10	dawdled 10
rancor 11	docile 11	spasms 12	dwindling 13
desperation 14	disheveled 14	improvising 17	sallow 18
ravenous 19	oblivious 19	cowered 20	mangy 24
compassionate 24	wrath 26	paltry 27	imperceptible 29
desolate 29			

Discussion Questions and Activities:

1. Who tells the story? *(Josh, a fifteen-year-old son of a Polish immigrant)*

2. What is Josh's family situation, membership and prospects? *(The family of five includes Josh, 2 parents, an older half-sister Kitty, and a younger brother Joey. The family is very poor and the situation seems to be getting worse.)*

3. Why doesn't the family apply for welfare or get help from their church or friends? *(There is no welfare system and the church and friends are also impoverished. It's a time of worldwide depression.)*

4. What is the mood of the chapter? Why? Cite examples from the text to support your answer. *(Answers will vary.)*

5. What is Josh's relationship to each of the other characters introduced in the chapter?

   Joey: Younger brother who idolizes Josh but whom Josh resents mildly because Joey was born frail and garnered a lot of attention and care

   Father: Once a proud man, now unemployed and resentful, who in anger lashes out at his family

   Mother: Provides the income, tries to keep everyone calm, supports her husband though she can see his unwarranted attacks

   Howie: Best friend who shares love of music

Kitty: Older half-sister who tries to help but loses her job

Miss Crowne: Supportive, caring teacher who enjoys Howie and Josh's musical efforts

6. Identify these details from the book and explain their significance.

    Banjo—Howie's prized possession

    Piano—had to be sold

    Ironing—the way the mother earns money

    School assembly—chance for Howie and Josh to appear and entertain

    Jigsaw puzzle—Howie steals it to give to Joey

    Five-cent milk bottle—Joey bought it to feed a stray cat

    More potatoes—Josh's request which leads to his father's verbal attack

7. Notice how many references there are to music in the chapter.

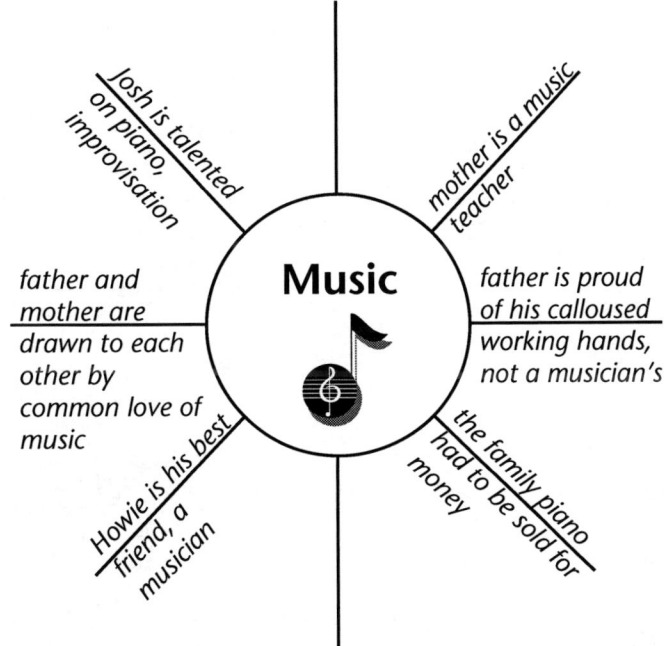

8. Look for contrasts in the chapter.

    Page 7—Joey is frail but tough.

    Pages 9-10—The piano-playing, culturally astute mother works ironing.

    Pages 13-14—The father, proud of pulling himself up by his bootstraps, is now unable to find work.

    Page 18—Howie's humor and his pitiful home life

    Page 21—Howie and Josh's beautiful music and the bread lines

9. Explain the personification on page 19. *(Nature is spoken of as though it is a human person.)*

10. What is Josh's decision at the end of the chapter and how does he come to the decision? *(He'll move out. His increasing disagreements with his father lead him to the decision, lest there be a sharper tragedy.)*

11. Predicting: What exactly does "getting out" mean for Josh? What will he do and where will he go? What are his prospects? How will he survive?

Supplementary Activities:

1. Examine the character of Josh's father. What are his good and bad points?

Good	Bad
•cares for his wife •proud of his efforts •hard-working	•angry •lashes out at children •critical of music •hypercritical of children

    Summarize the man's character in one sentence.

2. Talk to someone who was alive in 1932. What were the conditions?

3. Do some research on 1932. Look at history references and newspapers.

4. Start a bulletin board of images and events from the time and places in the book.

Chapter Two—Pages 31-45

Plot Summary:
Josh meets Howie at the corner drugstore and tells of his plans to hit the road. Howie decides to go along and in the midst of their excited planning, Joey appears and convinces Howie and Josh to take him along. They manage to set out, try panhandling, and eat a good meal with the proceeds. They plan to hop a train heading west but are put off in the morning by a railroad bull. Met by a wall of men with clubs and pitchforks they try to jump the next train but Howie is thrown down on the tracks by an express train on the next track.

Vocabulary:

| remnants 35 | arpeggio 36 | gloated 36 | absurdity 37 |
| loiterers 38 | agile 40 | withered 41 | savagery 43 |

Discussion Questions and Activities:

1. What is Josh's mood when he meets Howie at the corner drugstore? *(He is bitter because he feels rejected by both parents. He announces his plan to hit the road.)*

2. Why does Howie decide to join Josh on the road? *(His home life is bad. Also, Josh is his best friend.)* How does Howie's decision change Josh's mood? *(The boys become excited, planning for their adventures on the road.)*

3. What about Joey? *(Joey follows Josh from the house and then begs to be taken along when the boys leave.)*

4. Describe the boys' departure. *(They sneak away at night, taking along an old cardboard suitcase full of clothing, a remnant of a tattered blanket, and matches. There are no good-byes and no note of explanation.)*

5. How do the boys manage to buy hot dogs and a loaf of bread on their first day away? *(Joey and Howie panhandle for money.)*

6. What does Josh learn from a friendly hobo? *(the lowdown on the railroad detectives, which railroad is traveling west, help getting onto a freight train when the boys are thrown off into a hostile town and mob)*

7. What is the swelling roar the boys hear when they are turned off the train? *(a hostile crowd who intends to keep the boys and others out of their town)*

8. What happens to Howie at the end of the chapter? *(He doesn't leap onto the freight train in the best way and is thrown down the tracks.)*

Supplementary Activities:

1. There's a lot of anger in this book. Look for examples from the book.

2. How do you think Joey and Josh feel about Howie's death?

3. What is special about a story told in the first person? What other books have you read with a first person point-of-view? What do you need to remember in reading such books?

4. Conflict: Complete a conflict page for the book. (See page 17 of this guide.)

Chapter Three—Pages 46-63

Plot Summary:

The next afternoon Joey and Josh get off the train in a small town. They stay in an abandoned "house," drearier even than their home. The landlord arrives with his wife who gives the boys a meal and some potatoes for the road. An even hungrier gang takes the potatoes and even the potato the boys are cooking over a fire for dinner. Banged up from the fight with the gang, Josh is warned against fighting by the local police who do let the boys sleep in the jail overnight.

The Nature of Conflict

As is true in real life, the characters in novels face many conflicts. When two people or forces struggle over the same thing, conflict occurs. The excitement in novels develops from the use of the three main types of conflict: (1) person against person; (2) person against nature or society; and (3) person against himself or herself.

Below list some of the conflicts from the novel. In the space provided, briefly describe the conflict and indicate which type of conflict is involved, writing "PP" for person vs. person, "PN" for person vs. nature or society, and "PS" for person vs. self. Then choose three of the conflicts and describe how each was resolved.

Conflict	Description	Type

Conflict #1 resolution: _____

Conflict #2 resolution: _____

Conflict #3 resolution: _____

Vocabulary:

hostile 46	ravine 48	agony 48	contempt 49
cesspool 50	ramshackle 50	debris 51	ravenous 52
elation 52	pallet 53	callous 54	danged 56
extravagant 61	venom 62		

Discussion Questions and Activities:

1. Look over the fourteen identified vocabulary words. What do most of the words have in common? *(They are used to describe negative and unpleasant situations.)* What do they say of the book's mood and Joey and Josh's plight? *(It is bad, unpromising, and downcast.)*

2. What is reality for Josh and Joey in Chapter Three? Find specific examples from the text. *(Howie is dead, Josh is fearful of panhandling [page 46], advice is to return home [pages 48 and 56], the boys are grieving [page 47], the boys cry together [page 49], the boys are too proud to return home, there are drearier places than their slum home [page. 51, the ramshackle farmhouse they find], heat provides comfort [page 51, Joey almost embraces the stove], others were hungrier and worse off than Josh and Joey [page 62, note the "thugs" who stole the potatoes])*

3. It's said that there's some joy in every situation. What positives are there in this chapter for Josh? *(Joey wants to take the chance with him; finding the ramshackle farmhouse, white rooster, and stove; eating with the farmhouse owner and his wife; being allowed to sleep in the jail.)*

4. Which characters have you met so far in the book with names? *(only Josh and family, Howie, Miss Crowne, Josie, Ben)* Why doesn't the author give names for the others? *(Answers vary. Reader infers that these other characters aren't important to the plot as individuals, only taken together as a general impression.)*

5. What do Josh and Joey experience in a ramshackle farmhouse? *(warmth, meal from the white rooster, and then a meal with the house's owners)*

6. Why do Josie and Ben have names? *(Josie is kind to the boys, prepares a meal, engineers an upbeat noon meal with singing and music, and Ben gives them potatoes to take with them.)*

7. How is the boys' comfortable camping along the road disturbed? *(A gang of hungry fellows fights with them and takes their potatoes.)*

Supplementary Activities:

1. List the identified vocabulary words. Supply a word of opposite meaning and a neutral word for each. For example, hostile—bland—euphoric; contempt—neutrality—honor.

2. Opposites—Ying and Yang: Select five events from the book. Then imagine an opposite event from the book or one of your own imagination.

3. What is the conflict or problem in the book? Record on a story map. (See page 8 of this guide.)

4. Suggest titles for the first three chapters in the book.

Chapter Four—Pages 64-81

Plot Summary:
The situation gets so bad that Josh is thinking of nothing but food. He resorts to scavenging in garbage cans and panhandling. The brothers survive but it is a pitiful existence. Their luck seems to be changing when they stop at a tiny Nebraska farmhouse and a kindly old lady offers them baths, washes their clothes, and gives them stamped envelopes to write home. When Lonnie picks them up for a ride in his truck, heading south, their luck continues on the road upward. A waitress, hearing Josh play the piano, suggests that they look for her cousin who is running a carnival near Baton Rouge, Louisiana.

Vocabulary:

acclaim 64	capricious 65	humiliation 66	indignity 66
balm 68	slacken 72	drone 73	

Discussion Questions and Activities:
1. How have Josh's interests and concerns changed as he's on the road? *(Previously, he had many dreams and aspirations, but now he thinks only of food.)*

2. What are the various indignities and humiliations which Josh endures in Chapter Four? *(He really wonders if he and Joey will survive. He fights with rats for food from garbage cans. He and Joey beg for food, going house to house.)*

3. Identify these details from the chapter.

Bath	*first bath since they left home, at a small farmhouse in Nebraska*
Stamped envelopes	*given to Joey to write home from time to time to let the parents know that the boys are safe*
Lonnie	*a kindly truck driver who gives the boys a ride*

Old piano, "ain't no Steinway" (p. 78)   *piano in a diner that Josh plays and demonstrates his talent*

Bellyache   *what Lonnie's son died of—appendicitis*

4. How have Josh's thoughts changed from the beginning to the end of the chapter? *(At the onset Josh is thinking only of food, by the end he has reason to hope that there may be a chance for Joey and him at a carnival near Baton Rouge.)*

5. Why do Josh and Joey stay only one night in any place? *(For those on their own with no money and living on other's charity, they can only ask and expect food and/or shelter for one night.)*

Supplementary Activities:

1. What is Maslow's Hierarchy of Needs? Investigate the idea and then apply it to the book.

2. Compare Joey and Josh at home, on the road, and then compare to what you know of ten and fifteen-year-olds in your town.

Home	On the Road	In Your Town
•anger and unhappiness •school •dreams •music •sports •books •occasional movie •food daily •girls	•no dreams •no hopes •no interests except in finding food to eat	

3. What have you learned about Lonnie thus far? Record on an attribute web.

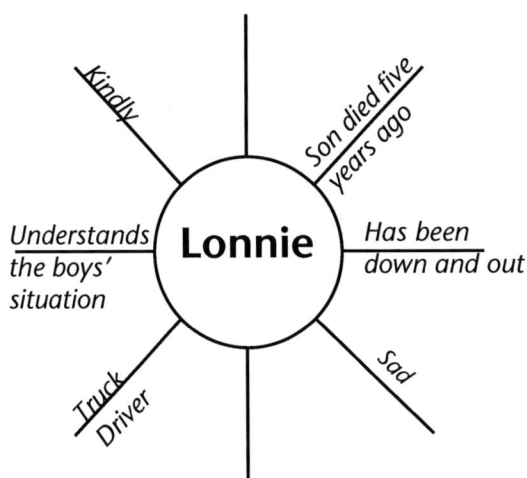

20

Chapter Five—Pages 82-105

Plot Summary:
Lonnie manages to find the carnival and Pete Harris reluctantly offers Josh a job playing the piano and ballyhooing outside the girlie show. Josh and Joey will receive board and room and $5.00 per week. The boys meet the group of carnies.

Vocabulary:

sustain 82	roulette 87	barkers 87	trounce 87
placard 88	syncopating 89	astride 90	nonchalant 90
rattlebrained 91	monotonous 93	obese 96	ingenuity 97
motley 98	interposed 100	ballyhooing 100	fervently 105

Discussion Questions and Activities:

1. Explain these phrases from the book: locate them in the chapter, explain with examples from the book and from your own experiences or those of others in other books. (Teacher Note: The stems are suggested answers only. Encourage and accept all answers.)

    position of a father (page 83)

    right to be boys (page 83)

    alien world (page 86)

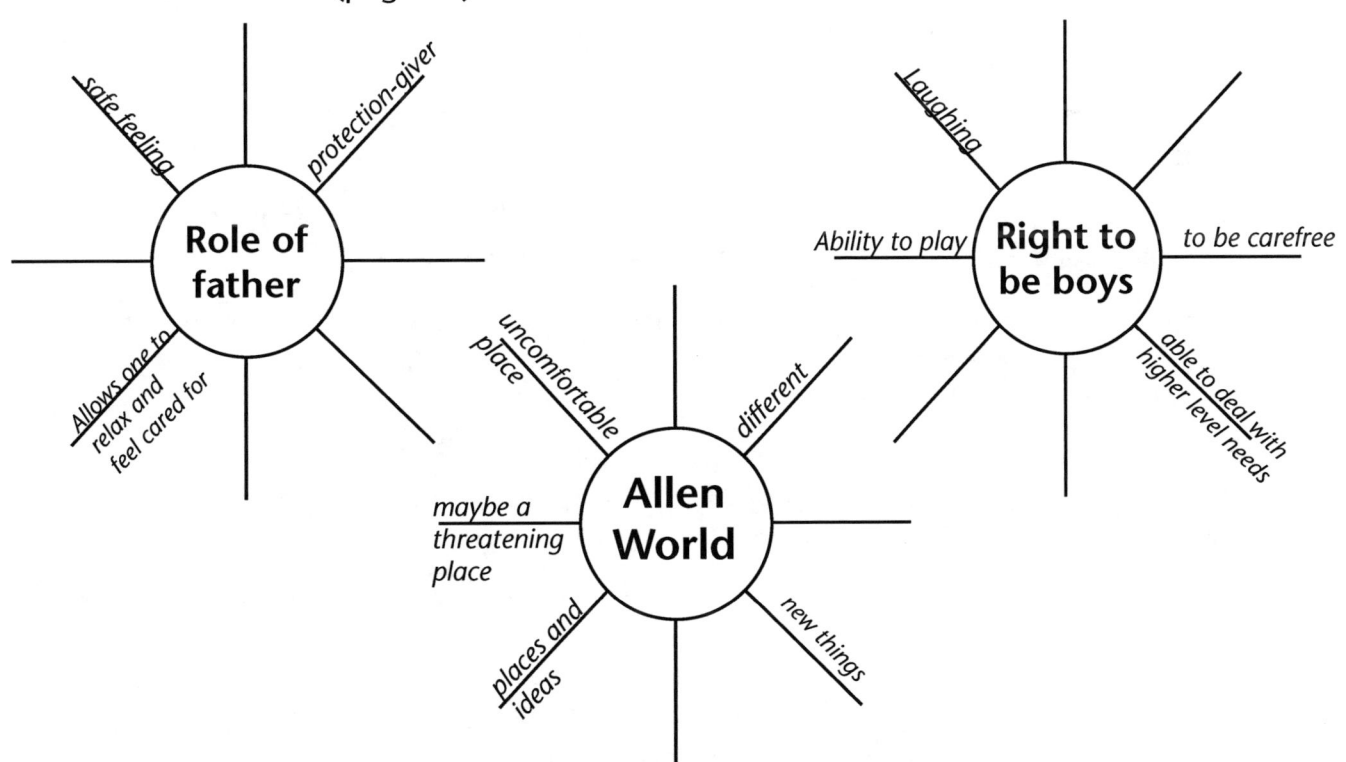

2. How does Josh's optimism return in the trip with Lonnie south? *(He keeps track of what Lonnie spends on the boys so he can pay him back later, is able to think of the future, smiles, music returns to his life, sleeps comfortably, and is well-fed.)*

3. Describe the scene when Josh first sees the carnival. *(page 87)* How is the scene different from anything Josh had seen before? How does he explain it? *(It reminds him of the amusement parks in Chicago.)*

4. How does Lonnie plead the boys' case with Pete Harris? *(He explains the referral from the waitress and is sympathetic to Harris's concern about affording any addition to the carnival. He urges an audition and lets the boys' appealing faces and music turn the day.)*

5. What is the deal that Pete offers Josh? *(room and board and $5 a week for playing the piano)*

6. Identify these characters from the carnival.

   Edward C   *a dwarf man who is direct and helpful to the boys*

   Blegan   *a dwarf man who is rattlebrained and gossipy and somewhat of a pest*

   Emily   *plays a clown in the carnival and is a big hit with the patrons; pretty, kind, and helpful*

7. How do Lonnie and the boys say good-bye? *(Lonnie is assured that Pete Harris will do right by the boys so he takes his leave, giving Josh a scrap of paper with his Omaha address and promising to stop to see them if he isn't laid off and returns to Louisiana. He promises to be ready to help if the boys get into a real jam.)* How do the boys feel after bidding Lonnie farewell? *(sad, bereft, not confident)*

8. How does Josh feel about the job? *(He's pleased to be earning the money but isn't exactly thrilled with the winking and ballyhooing part of the job.)*

9. What do you predict for Josh, Joey, and the carnival? Which of the carnies will prove important? Are there any parts in the story so far that may be foreshadowing for incidents yet to be told?

Supplementary Activities:
1. What is the carnival? Translate the word pictures in the book into a mural, poster, or an oral rendition.

2. What do you expect of a clown? Do you think that Emily will prove a spectacular attraction as a clown? Why?

3. On page 93, Josh talks about the monotonous sound of the carnival. What sounds have you experienced that could also be termed monotonous? Brainstorm some ideas with classmates and then choose one of the ideas to develop into a short descriptive paragraph.

4. Pattern Writing: Finish one of the following sentences from your own experiences.

    A father is _____. An alien world would be _____.

Chapter Six—Pages 106-128

Plot Summary:
Joey and Josh settle down to life with the carnival, happy that they can earn a little money. Joey and Josh send a few dollars to Lonnie in Nebraska, when he doesn't reappear in his truck, apparently laid off. Joey sends a couple dollars to his parents with a Christmas greeting, but Josh can't bring himself to sign the letter also. Through all of this, Josh is taken with Emily, the clown, even though she is fifteen years older than he is, has three children, and plans to marry Pete Harris. Josh becomes lonely, unable to accept Emily's motherly kindness. When the carnival burns, the outlook is much grimmer.

Vocabulary:

tormenting 106	pummel 106	clouted 107	dissuaded 115
scuttling 123	ominous 124	celluloid 124	smoldering 125
pavilion 125	despair 125	hysteria 127	

Discussion Questions and Activities:
1. How does Emily manage to be the star attraction of the carnival? *(She uses physical humor and interaction with the dwarfs to amuse the patrons. She works hard and long hours with constantly improvised situations.)*

2. Why is Josh attracted to Emily? *(Answers will vary. There are no girls his age nearby. Emily is pretty. She is also kind and takes an interest in the other carnival entertainers, especially Josh and Joey.)*

3. What is Josh's unforgiving streak mentioned on page 109? Give examples from the book to illustrate the streak. Is Josh justified? What advice would you give him? *(Josh won't write to his parents. He didn't leave a letter when he left home. He puts Lon Bromer's name on his identification card for emergencies. He doesn't talk about his father. He remembers his father harsher than may be warranted. Answers will vary on his justification and the advice.)*

4. How does Emily deal with Josh's growing fondness for her? *(She is understanding, doesn't laugh at him, but is clear that she plans to marry Pete Harris.)*

5. How is Christmas a bittersweet occasion for Josh? *(Emily invites some of the carnies to get together for Christmas Eve and they sing carols while Josh plays. Gifts are exchanged. Josh resents Pete Harris's inclusion in the party and seeing Pete and Emily as a couple.)*

6. Why is Josh sorry about his choice of gift for Emily? *(He goes along with Edward C. and Joey to give Emily polished dimes in a nicely wrapped box. He had wanted to give her something less practical and more personal and feminine. He is particularly unhappy when he sees Pete Harris's gift of earrings.)*

7. How does the long unhappy evening of Christmas Eve become long unhappy weeks for Josh? *(He has the blues and continues to be unhappy about Emily and Pete Harris. In his unhappiness, he continues to be angry, rude, and unlikeable to those around him.)*

8. What is the final unhappiness of the chapter? *(The carnival burns down.)*

9. Predicting: How will the carnies cope with no carnival? What will become of Josh and Joey?

Supplementary Activities:
1. What is a star attraction in carnivals or other events you've attended? Describe in a short paragraph.

2. The clown Bongo relies on physical humor to entertain. Try to dramatize the character of Bongo. Feel free to expand to other situations than just those described in the book.

3. How can a boxcar be a home? Brainstorm and record on attribute webs these two ideas: What kinds of places have you seen or read about that could be called homes? What makes a house or shelter a home?

4. At the end of the chapter Josh sums up the carnival time as a time when love was new and bewildering and bitterly sweet. Critique his words. Tell if he summarized well and why. How would Josh title Chapter Six?

5. If you could give Josh some advice, what would it be? Write a letter to him.

Chapter Seven—Pages 129-151

Plot Summary:
Joey and Josh take their leave from Baton Rouge, determined to travel to Nebraska to hook up with Lonnie, the truck driver who befriended them and helped them find the carnival. The trip north is rugged, especially after they lose Josh's twenty dollars in a store where they buy overshoes. Josh privately wonders whether this trip to Lonnie is a good idea after all.

Vocabulary:

riddance 132	hooch 139	contorted 141	complacent 141
notorious 142	counterfeit 146	misdemeanor 146	patronizing 147
humiliation 149			

Discussion Questions and Activities:

1. The first part of the chapter deals with different reactions to **worry** and **parting** as the carnies react after the fire. Generate some ideas about worry and parting, recording the variety of reactions of the characters in the book, as well as other ideas you've experienced personally, read in other books, or heard about.

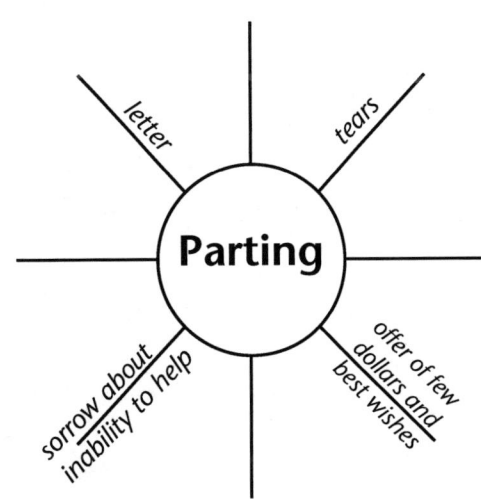

2. How does the author summarize Josh's feelings about what to do after the fire? *(page 131 "had to leave")* Is Josh's decision reasonable, advisable, appropriate? Can you understand it? What would you do in similar circumstances?

3. As the boys travel north to Nebraska, they encounter some of the "rhetoric of discontent." What ideas do they hear? *(pages 133-136, anger, unhappiness, urgency, desire for change, revolution, dissatisfaction)*

4. Who is Charley and how does he lead to the money disaster? *(Charley is a small time hoodlum whose bragging ways punctuate the ride he gives the boys. When he wants change for a twenty to pay a bill, Josh changes the bill. But then Josh is swindled out of his money in a shoe shop because he only has the one bill.)*

5. How did the author describe the shoe shop to foreshadow the dire event that occurs there? *(Pages 144-146, The proprietor is sour-looking and the shop has a smelly, vile air about it.)* How does Josh lose his money in the shoe shop? *(When he presents a twenty dollar bill to pay for overshoes, the proprietor takes the bill, accuses Josh of stealing it, and then declares it was counterfeit. He hails a passerby whom he addresses as sheriff and they agree the bill is counterfeit and then he threatens to charge Josh with a misdemeanor and put him in jail and Joey into a detention home if there is one yip out of the boys.)*

6. How do the boys fare as they proceed nearer to Lonnie? *(worse and worse—undernourished, tired, and with no prospects for improvement)*

Supplementary Activities:

1. What kind of decisions do the boys make? Look at the Decision-Making Chart on page 27 of this guide to evaluate. Choose a couple of the decisions that the boys make to evaluate with the chart. What alternatives do they have?

2. Do some investigation of the times described in the book: bootlegging operations, Prohibition, Franklin D. Roosevelt, and worldwide depression.

3. Compare life for a child in 1932, 1962, and 1992. Use the book for information, interviews with parents or grandparents, and your own experiences.

4. Writing Ideas:
   ✍The title of the book seems well-chosen;
   ✍The book is realistic, unrealistic;
   ✍Where do authors get their ideas for books, especially Irene Hunt?

Decision-Making Chart

Problem: State the chacter's problem in the book.

Solutions: Choose 3-7 possible solutions.
- (a.) State each choice in a short sentence.
- (b.) Design 3-5 "criteria" (questions you can ask to measure how good a particular choice may be)
- (c.) Rate the criteria for each solution: 1 =yes   2 =maybe   3 =no

CHOICES ↓	CRITERIA				
1.					
2.					
3.					
4.					
5.					
6.					
7.					

Chapter Eight—Pages 152-172

Plot Summary:

Joey and Josh make it to Nebraska in late February, exhausted, penniless, and hungry. As they make their way slowly to Omaha, Josh gets sicker and sicker, coughing, with a fever and very weak. He hides his condition from Joey, who does more and more of the pan-handling for food. When Josh berates Joey for giving away half a loaf of bread, there are harsh words and Joey leaves. Later Josh loses his way trying to find Joey and falls down in a field, sick and expecting to die. When he's rescued, the people find Lonnie's address in Josh's wallet and call Lonnie who comes to take the boy to his Omaha home. Josh starts recuperating but Joey is still missing. Lonnie promises to find the younger brother and alerts the police. Lonnie's niece Janey helps to care for Josh. Franklin Roosevelt is inaugurated.

Vocabulary:

quavering 153	tar-paper 153	desperation 157	seizure 158
constitution 164	inaugural 166	conversing 167	brooding 167
consecration 169			

Discussion Questions and Activities:

1. What is the nature of Nebraska in February, 1933, for Josh and Joey? *(It is very tough; the boys are cold, tired, and penniless. Their pitiful situation continues to be common.)*

2. How is the health of the boys? *(Joey continues to be healthy, but Josh has a bad cough and fever. The author doesn't detail a diagnosis, but it may be some kind of pneumonia-type illness.)*

3. How does a loaf of bread figure in the story? *(Josh is too sick to get up and Joey is given a loaf of bread. When Joey gives half of the loaf to a lady who had previously given the boys soup, Josh lashes out at him and Joey takes the banjo and his things and leaves.)* Is Joey justified in his actions? What about Josh?

4. How does Josh link up with Lonnie? *(When Josh falls down sick while looking for Joey and is found by some passerbys, they find Lonnie's address in Josh's wallet. Lonnie comes to pick up Josh and helps him begin to recuperate.)*

5. What does Josh remember as he is near death? *(He remembers his father rocking him during a childhood illness, the sense of security and warmth, and his father singing a Polish song of his own childhood.)*

6. Who is Janey? Is she homely or kind or young and naive? *(All of these ideas are expressed in Josh's thoughts. Janey is Lonnie's niece who lives next door to Lonnie with her grandmother. Janey helps in caring for sick Josh.)*

7. What is the significance of March 4, 1933? *(The inauguration of FDR. Janey and Josh listen to the inaugural address on the radio.)*

8. Predicting: What happens next in the story? There are three chapters left in the book. Will Joey be found? Will the boys be reunited with their parents? Will they survive?

Supplementary Activities:
1. What was the condition of medicine in 1933? Talk to some senior citizens who remember or investigate at the library. How would the treatment for Josh have changed from the time of the book to today?

2. Research the political situation in the United States in 1933. Who were the important figures? What were the various ways of thinking? What did the voters expect of Franklin Delano Roosevelt?

3. Why was the inauguration on March 4, 1933? How has the inauguration changed since 1776?

4. Choose one of these phrases from the book to discuss in a journal entry:

   •"I had heard that one's whole life passes before his eyes (when close to death)..." (page 159);
   •"The only thing we have to fear is fear itself..." (page 169);
   •"I don't know how long I stood there" (page 158);
   •"I've sinned against others as unfortunate as my own" (page 155).

Chapter Nine—Pages 173-190

Plot Summary:
Josh continues his convalescence. He gets to know Janey better and really likes her in a boy-girl kind of way. The search for Joey continues and Lonnie brings him "home" at the end of the chapter.

Vocabulary:
convalescence 173	lark 173	incredulously 178	astride 179
aped 179	aptitude 183	susceptible 185	dilapidated 185
relapse 186			

Discussion Questions and Activities:
1. What are Josh's dark moods (page 175)? *(He misses Joey, thinks about better times when they were younger and feels guilty and remorseful for losing Joey.)*

2. How does Janey deal with Josh's dark moods? *(She comes to visit the patient almost every afternoon after school. She makes him talk and tells him ideas about organized labor and other ideas.)*

3. How do earrings figure in the story? *(Josh had been entranced by Emily's earrings and how pretty she looked wearing them. When he first asked Janey about earrings, she was sure that they would look silly on her. She, however, does try them at the dime store, an indication of her interest in Josh and his ideas in a romantic kind of way. Later, Josh tells Janey that she doesn't need earrings; she is sweet and nice and pretty without them.)*

4. What are Lonnie's efforts to find Joey? *(He checks with police in various likely communities near Omaha, makes a phone call to the carnival folks, checks with detention homes, listens to the radio and reads the newspaper reports, and writes a letter to the boys' parents in Chicago.)*

5. What news is in the letter from Chicago? *(There is a letter to Lonnie and a separate letter for Josh from his mother; she relays her love and the news of the family and that Josh's father is unhappy about the situation with the boys; she asks for forgiveness and understanding.)*

6. How do they find Joey? *(Page 185, A radio report tells of a "half-famished angel with a shock of blond hair and an old banjo" from Chicago. Lonnie goes to the station and locates Joey, whom he brings home.)*

7. How does Josh greet Joey? *(shaking hands)* Why? *(It is in the pattern of behavior of a fifteen-year-old brother toward a ten-year-old younger brother.)*

Supplementary Activities:
1. What have you learned of Josh's character as the book continues? Add to your attribute webs. How has he changed?

2. Lonnie comments about Janey aping him. What do children learn from parents and other adults? What have you learned from your parents? Collect your ideas and then answer in a short paragraph.

3. On page 190 the author speaks of patterns of behavior. Define the term and then list some other patterns of behavior that you have observed or read about.

4. At the end of this chapter, a lot of people feel relieved. Brainstorm some ideas about relief and being able to sleep through the night. You may be able to include some similes.

answers to
questions

answers to
prayers

absence of guilt
or reduced guilt

Relief

able to stop
fixating on one
thing

comforted

Chapter Ten—Pages 191-213

Plot Summary:

Once Joey recovers and reunites with Josh, the boys visit Mrs. Arthur, the lady who had provided a home for Joey when he was discovered in the barn, frozen and malnourished. Josh plays on her grand piano, a magnificent instrument far finer than any he had played on before. Mrs. Arthur arranges an introduction to a restaurateur, Mr. Ericsson, who employs the boys as the "Wild Boys of the Road." Janey and Josh fall in love. Josh and Joey decide to go back to Chicago to be reconciled with their parents.

Vocabulary:

anguish 191	burrowed 195	remorse 195	compassion 196
pampering 198	resonant 203	churned 210	turmoil 211
repertoire 212			

Discussion Questions and Activities:

1. What is the nature of Lonnie and Josh's conversation after putting Joey to bed? (*There is a sense of contentment after finding Joey and ending the weeks of uncertainty about his fate. Lonnie details finding Joey. The man and the boy talk in the same room that Joey sleeps, unwilling to leave the sick Joey alone.*)

2. How does Josh handle the first night for a long time alone with Joey? *(He is afraid to go to sleep, he stays awake watching his brother and fixes milk and soup for him when he awakens during the night. The brothers talk and Josh gains an understanding of his own capacity to turn on others. He begins to understand his father's previous actions better.)*

3. As Josh sits awake and staring into the shadows, what picture becomes clear and sharp before him? *(He begins to understand his father's actions and wants to go home. He recognizes homesickness and a kinship with his father's sleepless nights, worrying about his sons as well as the remorse for past actions.)*

4. As the weeks of March pass by, what matters can Josh now think about? *(writing to Emily, getting a job, visiting at the Arthurs' home)*

5. How does Josh feel playing Mrs. Arthur's piano? *(He feels inspired; it was the finest instrument he had ever touched.)*

6. How does life change for Josh, as if a long nightmare has given way to a fairy tale? *(Page 205, Mrs. Arthur introduces him to a Mr. Ericsson who hires him to play at his restaurant. Joey and Josh are together in a warm, caring home and Josh has a paying job.)*

7. How do you think Lonnie feels about Josh and Joey being featured at the restaurant as the "Wild Boys of the Road"? *(The author doesn't tell us directly. She does describe Lonnie's eyes as angry when he hears about the promotion. He is probably unhappy and doesn't like for the boys to have their troubles be their drawing card, almost as freaks.)*

8. What kinds of love have been described in the book? *(romantic love between Janey and Josh, adoration of Emily by Josh, nurturing love of other humans as Gramma, Mrs. Arthur, Lonnie, Joey and Josh's parents)*

9. What happens when Josh and Joey sing their dad's old Polish song? *(The audience applauds as they never have before. Josh announces that they'll be going home to Chicago.)*

Supplementary Activities:
1. There is a lot of emotion in this chapter and this book. Pick out five or more incidents from the book. In a sentence or two explain the event and then suggest how the characters feel at that time.

2. When Josh is awake with Joey the first night they have been reunited, he sees a picture as clear and sharp. Is he describing a painting, photograph or picture, or is he describing something else? *(He is explaining that his feelings and understanding have cleared and they are now like a clear picture.)* Describe other "clear pictures" from your own experiences or from another book you've read.

3. Draw Josh's clear picture from page 195. Draw "clear pictures" from other books. Classmates will guess at the book from the picture. Answers can be noted on the reverse.

4. How might Josh and Joey be described as the lucky ones from the "army of homeless children" that roamed the countryside in the winter of 1933? Discuss with a classmate. Write a short paragraph to answer.

5. Compose letters from Josh to Emily and Kitty and Janey.

Chapter Eleven—Pages 214-223

Plot Summary:
Josh and Joey say goodby to Lonnie, Janey, Gramma, and the Arthurs. They travel by train (legally!) to Chicago. Mother, Dad, and Kitty meet them at the train station.

Vocabulary:

mohair 216	placards 218	defaced 218	aghast 218
callous 222			

Discussion Questions and Activities:
1. How do Josh and Janey part? *(They express love but are uncertain whether they'll reunite.)*

2. How is the trip home from Nebraska very different from the two previous trips to Nebraska? *(The first trip west was by train but Howie was killed and it was getting colder. The second trip to Nebraska from Baton Rouge was pitiful and starving, hitchhiking and walking as best they could. This trip home to Chicago from Nebraska is in warm weather, the boys are paying railroad customers and the boys can appreciate the countryside.)*

3. What do we typically mean when we say we're "starved"? *(We are hungry but hardly starving.)* How do Josh and Joey feel when Joey makes that comment? *(They are struck by his use of hyperbole in the common phrase now and that he never made the statement when he really was starving.)*

4. How do Josh and Joey feel as they anticipate the reunion? *(apprehensive, uncertain, scared)*

5. How is his father's behavior pattern like Josh's pattern in reunions? *(Both cry but turn their faces away to keep the emotion private.)*

Culminating Activities

1. Finish the story map and then explain how you feel at the end of the book? What is your recommendation for where to include the book in the school curriculum?

2. Review the character attribute webs and then cast the book for a movie. (See page 35 of this guide.)

3. Choose five adjectives, similes, or metaphors or other descriptive expressions to describe *No Promises in the Wind*. Defend your choices in a short paragraph.

4. Create a poster for the book.

5. Speculate about how the family will fare in the next ten years. Create letters which they might write to each other.

6. What does the title mean?

7. Writing Ideas: advice to the family as they reunite, why the Depression had such an impact on those who experienced it, etc.

Your Book Has Been Optioned for the Movies

1. You are the casting director. Who are the lead roles, supporting cast, and walk-ons? What kind of characters are they? What actors will fill the rolls? How should they look? What acting abilities will they need?

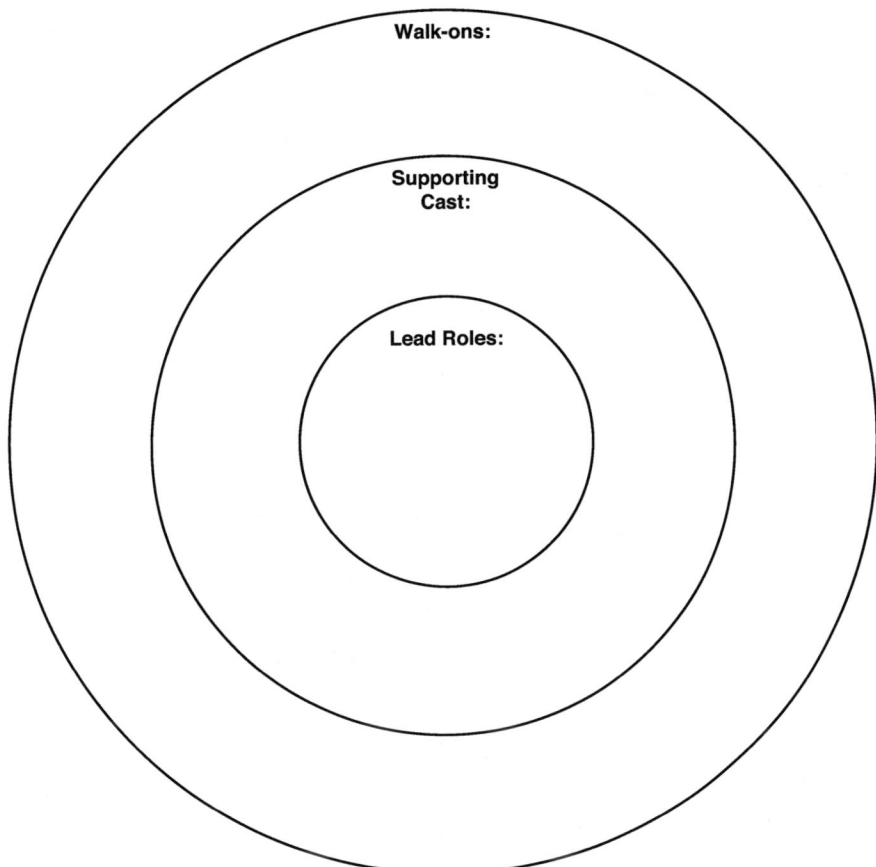

2. Design costumes for the cast. Explain your choices.

3. Pick the music. Will you need background music only or will you have musical "numbers"?

4. Design the set.

5. Identify and describe the props.

6. What will you title your movie? Why?

Assessment for *No Promises in the Wind*

Overview: Assessment is more than a single examination. The following ten activities can be completed during the novel study and submitted for review. Both teacher and student check the items as they are completed. Points may be added to indicate the level of understanding.

TEACHER	STUDENT		
_____	_____	1.	Keep a predicting chart as the book is read, revising and correcting as more is read.
_____	_____	2.	Complete three vocabulary activities from the list provided by the teacher. (See pages 4-5 of this guide.)
_____	_____	3.	Review the essentials of the plot with a comprehensive story map, board game, or multi-framed comic strip.
_____	_____	4.	How would the book be different if Joey were the storyteller? Answer in a short paragraph or two.
_____	_____	5.	Prepare a classmate for the book by giving advice about the best way to read it. Write it in a letter.
_____	_____	6.	Nominate the book and its characters for the Academy Awards. Support your choices in short paragraphs.
_____	_____	7.	Dramatize a significant part of the book.
_____	_____	8.	Write as though you were the author, explaining why you wrote the book.
_____	_____	9.	Prepare a ten-item true/false test for the book.
_____	_____	10.	Write a letter to your teacher praising or panning the book.